PRESENTATION AND COMMUNICATION SKILLS
A HANDBOOK FOR PRACTITIONERS

KAREN RAWLINS

First edition 1993

Published by
Macmillan Magazines Ltd
4 Little Essex Street
London WC2R 3LF

Companies and representatives throughout the world

Typeset by Graphic Ideas, London

Printed by
Spottiswoode Ballantyne Printers Limited
Colchester, Essex, UK.

ISBN 0-333-60960-3

For Ian and Emily Victoria

2 (

CONTENTS

INTRODUCTION

I am always willing to learn.
It's just that I don't like being taught
Winston Churchill

This Handbook aims to provide you with the necessary knowhow and skills to communicate effectively through presentations. It emphasises the presentation as a learning situation in which new or deeper understandings are being developed for some purpose.

Presentations by their very nature are more one way than two way. Nevertheless, this Handbook takes the view that even when one person is doing most of the talking, this can be done in a way that makes those listening feel that they are part of an active dialogue that is taking account of their needs and encouraging them to be responsive and to learn.

It is therefore the presenter's task to engage, enthuse, motivate, challenge and support in ways that facilitate effective communication and learning.

The techniques we will be considering are common to most types of presentation, such as a talk to your colleagues in a formal or informal learning or training situation, a slot in a business meeting or conference, or an after dinner speech. It will help you think about those with whom you wish to communicate, why you wish to communicate, the options open to you in improving your communication, and how you might gauge your effectiveness.

It will also help you deal with questions and answers following a presentation and in running group discussions. It looks at nerves and the 'awkward customer', which are always a challenge no matter how experienced we are. Throughout it will help you to think about the influence of the context within which you are giving your presentation and the alternatives open to you in presenting in different settings.

The degree to which an interactive approach is possible will depend on the nature and purpose of the presentation.

Sometimes you will be able to function more as a facilitator than a presenter, and this is taken into account in what follows.

The Handbook will largely mirror the structure followed when developing a presentation.

It will begin by looking at the planning process, including how to decide on your aim, setting objectives and selecting the most appropriate approach.

Having designed a structure, the practical issues of choosing, preparing and using resources are addressed in Chapter Two.

The next section covers presentation techniques and looks at how to start and close a session, as well as how to use your nerves positively.

Evaluation is an important element of any learning situation and Chapter Four explores the most common methods used.

Finally, you will be asked to consider how you will make use of the learning you have achieved by completing your own personal development plan.

The Activities throughout the text will help you to make sense of the information and ideas presented and to relate them to the kinds of situations in which you want to communicate effectively through presentations.

CHAPTER 1:
PLANNING AND PREPARATION

1.1 INTRODUCTION

If you fail to prepare, prepare to fail!

Everything we do involves some sort of preparation. If we go on a journey, for example, we normally have a destination in mind and a purpose for going. Since we generally know where we are before we set out, it is a relatively straightforward process to work out the most suitable route to take us there.

These in essence are the steps required when planning any type of presentation.

You first require an aim to establish a purpose or meaning for you the presenter, and also for your audience. By keeping your aims to the forefront of your mind during the planning process they can then be used as a filter for your content, thus ensuring that you keep on course.

If we continue to use the earlier analogy of the journey as a framework for planning we can see that we need to establish:

Where we are now:	Our starting point; for example, what your audience currently knows/thinks and feels about the subject.
Where we need to get to:	Our final destination or overall goals/aims; for example, what does your audience need to know/understand/do, and so on.
How we get there:	The route or 'teaching' content required to address the gap identified above.

A useful *aide-mémoire* to help guide you through the planning phase is the famous quote from Kipling:

I keep six honest serving men
(they taught me all I know)
Their names are What and Why and When
and How and Where and Who

In other words, we need to consider:
- The aim of the presentation (the *Why*)
- The content (the *What*)
- The audience (the *Who*)
- The learning method (the *How*)
- The learning environment (the *When* and *Where*)

We will be looking at each of these areas in detail in this book.

ACTIVITY

Recall a presentation that has been made to you recently. Think about your positive and negative feelings before, during and after the event. The following questions will help you to reflect. You may also have some questions of your own. You might find it useful to write down your thoughts so that you can refer back to them from time to time as you work through this book.

BEFORE YOU ATTEND THE PRESENTATION:
What, if any was the stated purpose of the presentation?
What did you intend to get out of it?

DURING THE PRESENTATION:
Content:
What did you think about the extent and nature
of the presentation?
How did the content meet your identified needs?
Apart from meeting your identified needs, how relevant and useful was it to you generally?

Presentation style:
What did you think about the presenter's style?
In what ways did s/he draw on your experience?
Describe any factors which stopped you from
listening and learning.

Environment:
In what ways did the presenter take into account the learning environment?

cont...

REFLECTING UPON THIS EXPERIENCE:
If you had been the presenter, what would you have done
the same, more of, less of, differently?
What are the three most important things you have learnt from
this experience?

1.2 ESTABLISHING YOUR AIM

*If you don't know where you're going
Any road will take you there*

Establishing your aim should be the first area you consider
when planning a presentation. Your overall aims should
influence everything you do. Without aims you run the risk
of designing an approach that is irrelevant or unrelated to
the needs of the learner. Some presenters are tempted,
however, either to decide on an aim after producing the
content or to produce a set of aims and then ignore them
completely. Where there is more than one person designing
the content, there is a particular danger of this happening.

An example of this occurred at a seminar held by a
company that produced management training programmes.
The seminar was attended by existing and potential clients
and was designed to market their products and explain how
to use the packages within an organisation's management
development structure.

An existing client had agreed to undertake the main
presentation but instead of promoting the actual product he
spent the entire time allocated to him talking about his own
company. This was not deliberate on his own part – he just
hadn't been made sufficiently aware of the main aim of the
seminar. Consequently, many delegates left during the
refreshment break and the company lost substantial sales as
a result.

So how do you go about deciding on your aim?

Whether you are presenting to a group of 250 or two, the same principles apply. You need to be clear about your aims. However, it is difficult to clarify your aims until you know something about those with whom you wish to communicate effectively. What are their needs? What will they be expecting to learn from you. What will encourage them to listen and what will put them off? If your aim is not shared by them, how will you make the bridge between the two so that they are encouraged to engage with your aim?

Ways of learning more about your audience's needs, interests and concerns are discussed in Section 1.4: 'Establishing your audience's needs'.

Defining aims

In formal training events, it is customary to specify in advance the aims and objectives of the session. These ensure a clarity of focus and provide a basis for monitoring and evaluating effectiveness. Listing specific objectives for a presentation may not always be appropriate to your setting or audience. Communicating your aim, however, is. This can be done in many ways. For example, at an after dinner speech, you might say at the beginning of your talk:

> What I want to do tonight is to tell you about my recent admission as an emergency patient in the NHS and, as a result of this experience, some of the key issues I think we need to address. I shall begin by .... and then go on to .... At the end of my talk I shall ....

At a team meeting you would probably be even more specific:

> The purpose of this presentation is to tell you about changes to the health and safety laws that will have a direct impact on us. By the end of this presentation and following discussion, my aim is to ensure that we all know what we need to do as individuals and as a group to bring these into practice.

ACTIVITY

Go back to thinking about your imaginary or real presentations. Think about the first three minutes. What might you say about your aim(s)? Drawing on your own experiences of presentations, what would 'communicating these effectively' at the beginning mean to you?

Your aim is intended to outline in broad terms the overall purpose of the learning event. It should also be measurable, related to the needs of the audience and achievable from the presentation.

We will be looking at each of these criteria in more detail in the next chapter.

ACTIVITY

Re-visit a previous training event you either ran or attended as a learner. How did the aims assist you in the learning process? In the light of this chapter would you change these aims and, if so, how?

1.3 SETTING OBJECTIVES

Once you have decided on your aim(s) for a session, it is sometimes useful and appropriate to set out some objectives for your presentation. These will be more specific than your aim(s) and can provide a very useful reference point to help people to review what you are doing and why.

Writing objectives

Whereas an aim is critical in any learning situation, you may not always feel it necessary to break this down further into a set of objectives. Your decision will probably be dictated by the type of event you have in mind and the broad aim itself. A short talk such as an after dinner speech or a presentation at a conference, for example, may require just a general aim. On the other hand, a 1½-hour session involving presentation and discussion and including a number of different teaching concepts will probably require specific objectives.

An example of a situation where a broad aim may be enough could be a talk given at an antenatal clinic on the role of the community midwife.

Alternatively, a second session at the same clinic to discuss safety in the home may have specific objectives as well as an overall aim.

Types of objectives

Objectives should provide clear guidelines to you and the learner as to the proposed content and outcomes of the learning experience; that is, what the learner will know or be able to do or understand.

Objectives tend to be written in terms that allow for evaluation of success, related to the needs of the learner and achievable from the presentation. They also usually set out a condition or circumstance.

They may cover a change in behaviour or performance (these are called behavioural objectives). Alternatively, they may specify the process by which you consider the learner will benefit from being involved. The latter objectives are called expressive objectives and can be used where you are seeking to change attitudes or promote understanding. In these circumstances it may not be possible to specify the objective in behavioural terms. An example of each type of objective is provided below.

A behavioural objective relating to a safety session could be:

- The learner will be able to describe accurately the company's evacuation procedure without reference to the fire code.

An expressive objective relating to a session on effective presentations could be:

- The learner will experience the frustration of having to cope with too many overhead slides and too much new information during a presentation.

The type of objective you use will normally depend on your overall aims and it could well be that you decide to use both in one learning event.

Fulfilling the criteria for writing objectives

Objectives need:

- *To be measurable* – clearly, unless an objective incorporates some sort of measure or standard you will be unable to assess whether it has been achieved. Measures can be quantitative (how much? how many?), qualitative (how well?) or specify timescales (by when?). You can include more than one type of measure within the same objective

- *To be achievable* – an objective needs to be realistic and possible to achieve as a result of the learning experience

- *To be relevant* – the objective must relate to the overall aim, which will in turn relate directly to the needs of the learner

- *To include a condition* – the objective should describe the circumstances or conditions that will apply when the objective is being measured; for example, with reference to notes, on a blank piece of paper, using a set of tables, working alone/without assistance.

ACTIVITY

Return to your real or imagined presentation. Would the writing of specific objectives be appropriate to this situation? If so, devise an aim and specific objectives. If not, think about another situation of your own, or the following example:

Devise an aim and objectives for a safety in the home session for new mothers at an antenatal clinic class.

Using the above example, you may have produced an aim along these lines:

The aim of this session is to reduce the risk of accidents to children by making new mothers more aware of the potential hazards within their own home and the safety measures available to avoid accidents occurring.

Specific objectives might include:

Following this session, the group will:

1.   State [the behaviour] the frequency [the standard] with which accidents, including fatalities, occur in the home environment [the condition].

This objective could be quantified as follows:

1.   Be able to describe the six most common hazards within the home and the safety measures that could be taken to avoid their occurring.
2.   Be able to undertake accurately a safety audit within their own home.

However these are only *examples* of the type of objectives you could use. Your own set may look entirely different even though the content may cover the same things. Using language you and your learners are comfortable with is as important as ensuring that the aim is fully incorporated within the objectives.

Can you recognise the advantages of breaking down the aim in this way?

ACTIVITY

Return to the Activity with which this chapter began when you remembered your own experience of a presentation (p4). How would you have written objectives for that event? What are the advantages of breaking them down as described above?

If you have broken your aim down into objectives that specify clearly the main learning outcomes necessary, it is a relatively straightforward process to produce a presentation plan that does not deviate from your overall aim. Objectives can also give your audience real clarity regarding what they can expect to achieve as a result of your presentation.

Overcoming obstacles in writing objectives

Writing objectives can be difficult sometimes, and many presenters find the inclusion of measures particularly problematic. In situations where tangible outcomes are sought, for example from a sales training presentation, it is a fairly straightforward process. When there are less tangible goals, such as where you are seeking to change attitudes, producing appropriate objectives may be more challenging.

However, there are very few, if any, situations where objectives and measures cannot be produced. If you think about it, there must be a clearly identified need for your presentation to have been considered in the first place. As such, something needs to be achieved or changed and this is your objective.

Visualising outcomes

A useful technique for helping you decide on what measures to use is visualisation. This is a basic problem-solving technique you can employ in any situation where you are having difficulty finding a solution. It involves your picturing learners who have successfully achieved your aim and objectives. You analyse in detail what it is that tells you this. These factors could be the measures you are looking for.

The sorts of questions you could ask yourself might be:
- How has the learners' behaviour changed?
- What can they do now that they couldn't do before?
- What are the learners now thinking about the subject, and what were they thinking before?
- How are they feeling? How has this changed from what they were feeling before?

ACTIVITY

Think back to your imagined or real presentation. Visualise at the end of your session two different people in that group coming up to you and saying: 'What an effective presentation.' Now visualise, if that were so, how you would expect their behaviour to have changed. What would they be able to do that they could not do before? What will they be thinking about the subject now that they were not thinking before? How are they feeling? How has this changed from what they were feeling before?

Maybe not all of these visualisations could be expected to give you measures that are appropriate, but at least one could be expected to result from your presentation.

ACTIVITY

Return to the previous Activity. Are there ways in which you could improve your objectives as a result of this reflection?

1.4 ESTABLISHING YOUR AUDIENCE'S NEEDS

You are there because of your audience. Getting to know your audience is vital if you are to communicate effectively and enable learning to take place.

This may seem rather obvious but it is not as easy as it sounds. It is difficult sometimes to respond to your audience's needs, especially if it means skipping areas that you find particularly interesting or useful! However, once you allow the subject to dominate the learning rather than the learners, you can seriously reduce the effectiveness of the communication process.

ACTIVITY

Think back to being on the receiving end of a particular presentation and to your reflections in the Activity at the beginning of this chapter (p4). How well were your needs, interests, experiences and concerns taken into account by the speaker?

How have you felt/would you feel if a speaker seemed to be meeting his/her needs rather than yours?

Think of specific ways in which presenters have communicated their interest in you to you.

Failing to consider your audience can result in the learner being:

Alienated: if you offend their value system

Insulted: if you fail to recognise their existing knowledge and experience and pitch the learning event at an inappropriate level

Confused: if you assume a level of expertise that isn't there

Bored: if you fail to relate the subject to their needs

Patronised: if you use an inappropriate style.

All these feelings will be counter-productive and interfere badly with the learning process.

ACTIVITY

Think about a stranger coming into your work environment to make a presentation to you and your colleagues. Imagine that she is an expert on something that is going to be important for you in the near future. What would she need to take into account in planning and delivering her presentation?

You may have included some of the following in your answer:

- *The learners' needs, interests, feelings, concerns in relation to the subject matter* – this is the most important factor of all

- *The size of the group* – this will affect the choice of visual aids, room layout and also tuition methods. Someone speaking to a large audience will also need to consider the use of a microphone

- *The current level of knowledge and experience* – what does the audience know already? At what level can the learning event be pitched? Is there a mixture of abilities, and if so how will these be dealt with? Will specialist terms or jargon be able to be used? Can the content be related directly to the audience's experiences?

- *The audience's status* – how junior/senior? Is there a mixture? (This may have major implications for the speaker, particularly if staff and managers are together.) Will a particular approach need to be adopted? (This could influence the choice of dress or presentation style.)

- *Inter-relationships* – do the group members already know each other? Are there any internal politics or hidden agendas that it is important to be aware of? Are there any members of the group likely to cause problems? How could these be dealt with? Are there any external developments that will affect the group and that the speaker should know about beforehand?

- *Pre-conceived ideas/likely values* – what will the group's attitude be to the speaker and the subject? How will they perceive the group's aims, expertise and experience? Are the members there out of choice? What will their motivation levels be? How could these attitudes be dealt with? Are there any particular attitudes that need to be brought into the open/addressed?

- *Preferred learning styles* – will the learners respond better to a practical session or a more theoretical presentation? How can you cater for the different learning styles of the group?

In situations where you already know your audience or are able to meet them beforehand, it will be relatively simple to establish their needs. Wherever possible, you should try to involve all, or a representative sample of, participants in identifying appropriate aims for the presentation. Where this is not possible, you may have to rely on secondary sources for information and this may not always be forthcoming. It might be useful if you can speak to a sample of attendees in situations like this and, at the very least, insist that your questions regarding the audience profile are answered. After all, you will probably be the one who gets the blame if things go wrong so you have every right to expect as much help as possible.

Additional sources of help may also be useful. These could come from any or all of the following:
- Your manager
- Colleagues
- A subject matter expert
- Previous presenters
- Someone who knows the group.

1.5 GATHERING YOUR MATERIAL

Selecting the right content will be a relatively straightforward process if you have carefully developed your aims and objectives beforehand and thought about your audience.

However, as time will normally be restricted, difficulties often arise over how much content it is possible to cover in the time available. Many new presenters worry about either covering all their material too quickly or running out of time. With experience this becomes less of a problem and structuring your notes to enable you either to cut out sections or add supplementary material will overcome any difficulties.

Before we can look at how to structure your presentation, however, we need to look at the ways in which you can gather your material.

Deciding on the content

Even if you feel that you have all the information you need at your disposal, you need to consider whether there is merit in double checking it is up-to-date. This will involve checking the facts and current views or opinions relating to them.

It may be, for example, that new developments or thinking are influencing current opinion on your subject and that this needs to be reflected in your presentation. You may also derive benefit from undertaking some supplementary reading so that you have confidence in your subject knowledge.

ACTIVITY

Think about a topic on which you might give a presentation to your own colleagues. How would you set about preparing yourself for dealing with the content? How would you ensure that you are up to date and in tune with current developments?

Now imagine a topic in which you are interested but know little about. What would you need to find out and how would you do this?

There are many ways of preparing yourself but the best place to start is with yourself. If you begin your research by tapping into your own experiences, views and knowledge your ideas will not be clouded or influenced by anyone else's.

Other sources of information could include:

- *Newspapers, trade magazines and journals* – recent publications will obviously be more up-to-date than most textbooks and will provide you with an indication of new or current thinking

- *Libraries* – books are an obvious source of material but you need to check they are up-to-date and that the content is well-researched and appropriate to your needs

- *Existing teaching notes* – these can be highly comforting to have at your disposal, particularly if you don't feel very confident about structuring your notes or with the subject matter itself

- *Other people* – who can you talk to about this subject? Who do you know who may know others with whom you might talk? It is easy to assume that your questions may be an intrusion for others, but it is surprising how easily and pleasantly people respond to such requests, particularly if you show yourself to be a keen learner and a good listener

- *Your boss and colleagues* – other people can be useful in a variety of ways. You can use them to discuss ideas and to benefit from their expertise and experience. They can also provide you with additional reference sources and materials

- *Procedure manuals, circulars and correspondence* – these will often provide you with the latest information on a particular subject or your company's latest policies and procedures.

There is a danger that once you have viewed someone else's approach you find it difficult to utilise your own ideas and personality to the full. This is why it is helpful to brainstorm your own ideas before looking at other resources.

In addition, it is important that you don't automatically assume that someone else's approach is necessarily good or that it is right for your particular learners.

When looking at any existing material it is always useful to ask yourself a number of questions, such as:

- Was the learning a success?
- Did it achieve its overall aims and objectives?
- Was the material written for a similar audience?
- Do the aims and objectives conform with the learning needs you have identified for your own learning event?
- Is the content up-to-date? Is it appropriate for your own particular circumstances and your intended audience?

Once you feel confident with the subject matter required for your presentation, the next step will be for you to assemble this into some sort of structure. How you prepare your presentation outline will very much depend on the particular situation and circumstances to which you are responding.

1.6 SELECTING THE MOST APPROPRIATE APPROACH

I hear and I forget
I see and I remember
I do and I understand
(Chinese proverb)

There are a variety of communication methods available to you within a presentation. In the majority of cases there is no one right approach and you may find that you use different ways to cover the same aims with equal success. Whatever approach you use, it should be one you feel confident with.

There are principally two main modes of presentation:

Presenter-led or-centred

This is where the presentation process will be from the presenter to the group. This method is normally used to present information, for example, a lecture or conference speech.

Audience-or learner-centred

This approach involves the learners discovering or applying learning points for themselves with the presenter facilitating the process.

It may seem strange to speak of a presentation as a potential learner-centred situation. However, even with large audiences, it is still possible to involve the group and take account of their experience when developing the structure of your presentation.

The degree to which you use either approach will depend on a number of different factors.

ACTIVITY

What factors would lead you to select either method of instruction? Can you identify specific examples of when you would use each of them?

cont...

Think about different kinds of presentations you have experienced in large and small groups. Can you think about the different approaches that have been adopted? Try to remember their different effects on you. What were some of the factors that made one style more appropriate or effective than another?

The degree to which the effective communication of content involves the translation of new knowledge, skills and attitudes will normally influence your choice of approach quite considerably.

Where there is a large amount of knowledge to be imparted you may, for example, need to consider more of a presentation-centred approach, such as a lecture. However, this doesn't have to be the case and it may be that you decide to use the time that you have available to check understanding rather than to input new information.

By sending out pre-presentation reading material, for example, you are able to cover much of the knowledge input beforehand, which leaves you free to offer a more participative or reflective presentation involving group discussions or activities.

Where you are speaking at a conference and reflecting on personal experience you may not choose to do this, but it may still be worth considering as it could release you to discuss in more depth the application or implications of the subject area.

It is not always possible to send out material prior to a presentation but it is worth considering. Sometimes this requires negotiation with others, such as when you are invited in by a team to make a presentation on an area in which you are considered highly knowledgeable. Sending out material beforehand will also allow your audience to:

- Assimilate information at their own pace. Where there are areas of difficulty this is of particular value as it will enable them to revisit the same information as many times as they need, before and after your presentation

- Identify those areas where they require further help and clarification, thereby allowing an effective use of discussion or question and answer time

- Analyse critically the information during the presentation (rather than simply concentrate on absorbing the facts)

- Focus, together with you, on the application of the information

Furthermore, if material is sent out beforehand you will be able to adopt a more audience-centred approach.

Remember the Chinese proverb at the beginning of this section? As the audience will be seeing the information they should find it easier to remember the facts.

Your presentation can then help them to consolidate their understanding of the learning points within it.

ACTIVITY

Imagine yourself doing a presentation on a subject you feel confident about. Imagine different audiences and aims for your presentation, and the approach that you would take for each. What are the advantages of the approaches you have selected? Now think about using an alternative approach for each. How might your audience have reacted?

Where your presentation seeks to change attitudes, an interactive approach will be the most suitable. By holding group discussions within your presentation, for example, you will be encouraging people to reflect on what you have said and to exchange ideas and opinions with other group members.

Presentations are not really appropriate for skills development although they may be used to some extent as part of a learning plan. However, you cannot teach a new skill simply by telling people how to do something. They may, for example, buy a book on how to play golf, or watch a golf professional on television or at the golf club, but it is only when they pick up the club themselves and have a coach to facilitate their skill development that any real progress can be made.

Your choice of approach will also be influenced by the time and resources you have available.

Certain activities are more time consuming than others and where time is limited this may prevent you from taking as learner-centred an approach as you would like.

Group activities and discussions tend to take longer than a presentation, so you may have to use a more trainer-centred approach for some areas in order to release time for group discussions on others.

Availability of space and the size of the group are also important considerations.

Clearly you will need more room for certain activities than others and you should take this into account during the planning stage. This in turn will affect your choice of visual aids.

Finally, remember that you must be competent in whatever method you choose and feel comfortable using it.

1.7 STRUCTURING YOUR NOTES

Having decided on your strategy and gathered all your material, you are finally ready to begin writing the actual content of your presentation.

There are a number of different ways in which you can approach this and we will be looking at a selection of these later on. Before we consider the actual format of your notes, however, we need to look at how to structure the material that you have collected.

Irrespective of the type of presentation, having an overall structure is very important for the successful achievement of your aims and objectives.

ACTIVITY

Think of a time when you have attended a poorly structured presentation. How did this make you feel? What impact did it have on the effectiveness of the speaker's communication with you and

cont...

...cont

also on your willingness to engage with their content? How did you know, in terms of what the speaker did or did not do, that the material was badly structured?

Now think of times when you felt that a talk was very well-structured. What were the main differences? Jot down some key learning points from your reflections.

Most of us need a clear idea as to the focus of the presentation in order to remain interested. A well sign-posted structure will distinguish between the main and supplementary messages and will ensure that the session does not over-run. Running over time is one of the easiest ways you can lose or antagonise your learner.

A well-structured presentation will normally have:

- *A logical sequence* – not necessarily starting the subject at the beginning but a sequence that the learner understands and makes sense

- *Regular sign-posting* – this is where we've been/ this is where we're going next

- *Regular summaries* – a summary of the learning points/ main messages just covered. This enables the audience to check their understanding and to consolidate what you are saying

- *Built in monitoring or reviews* – to check that the objectives you intended are being met and that there is understanding of the material covered

- *An introduction, main body and conclusion* – a well-known phrase illustrates this well. You should:

  Tell them what you're going to tell them.
  Tell them.
  Tell them what you've told them.

- *Key/main headings or learning points* – the number of main learning points you will include will depend on the

time available. To give you an example, a formal presentation should not involve more than five main headings. It is always better to cover a few points well than a number badly.

This last point is particularly important – there is a limit to how much information people can take in at any one time. Being over ambitious will simply result in your audience being overwhelmed and confused, although they might not convey this to you directly Many people feel shy or are afraid of appearing stupid, and are reluctant to admit that they do not understand something.

People are very uncertain about themselves and their abilities, particularly when in a group. Some of your audience might be feeling uncertain and anxious, particularly if they are being asked to contribute to a group discussion. It is critical that you constantly check to make sure that your learners are comfortable with the material covered so far.

Deciding on what to leave out can be one of the most difficult parts of preparing the content. This is particularly tough if it is a subject that you have a special interest in or knowledge of. Be selective, therefore, and filter all your material through the aims and objectives before finalising the actual content. If any content doesn't lead either directly or indirectly to the learners' achievement, it isn't relevant to include.

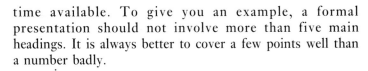

ACTIVITY

Make an attempt at learning the following number: 165196946615. Keep going until you can reproduce it on a separate page without looking.

What was easy about this for you? What was difficult? What helped you to succeed?

You will probably have adopted one of two methods:

(a)   You may have used association to remember some or all of it; for example, if you were born in 1969 this part would be easy for you to recall and you would therefore have broken the number down into:

165 1969 46615

(b)   If you had no such association, you would probably have broken the number down into groups of three or four numbers (or possibly twos).

You may have tried to learn the number without breaking it down but it is most unlikely that you would have found this easy. If you did manage to learn this way, repeat the exercise with another number (ask a colleague to provide you with the digits) and try learning it using either of the above methods – you should find it takes you far less time and effort.

So what does this exercise illustrate? It is designed to demonstrate what it is like to be a learner trying to absorb a body of new facts or information. Learning is much easier if it is dealt with in digestible chunks.

People need time to consolidate any new information or learning and this can best be achieved if it is provided in 'bite-sized' pieces rather than in one go. Breaking your presentation up into main headings will help achieve this, particularly if you also include reviews and summaries.

By structuring your presentation in this way, therefore, you are assisting the learning process.

ACTIVITY

Think about a real or imagined presentation, perhaps using the same one that you have used before in these Activities. What difficulties might you have in structuring this in ways that ensure effective communication and learning on the part of your audience? What will be hard to cut out, and why? What will be easy?

If there were three main things you want your group to remember or do differently, what would they be?

1.8 PREPARING YOUR CONTENT

You should already have your own method of organising your material, and if this works well for you we suggest you continue with it. However, the following checklist may be useful as it provides a logical structure to follow when preparing your material, whether the final result is a full script or a presentation outline.

Brainstorm your proposed main headings or learning points

This technique involves your writing down whatever ideas come into your head about the headings you should include. Don't try to analyse anything at this stage or you will interfere with the free flow of ideas.

Refine and select

Now revisit your list and filter each heading through the aims and objectives. Cross out anything that isn't relevant and then prune your ideas into the number of headings that you want to include. You may find that you need to collate some of the headings into one main area. You may not be able to cover some points in the time available, in which case you need to delete them. (You could perhaps keep this as supplementary information for use if there is time at the end of your presentation.)

Order

Your headings now need to be ordered in a logical sequence that includes an introduction and a conclusion. There are a number of ways that your content can be ordered. If you are talking about a specific process you can structure your presentation to reflect the stages involved.

Alternatively, you might order your material as a series of learning steps that take your audience towards a specific conclusion. This order may be preferable where the audience needs to understand one level before going on to the next.

If no particular order is required to make sense of your content then it is largely up to you how you structure your material.

The time of day may also inform your decisions. Avoid covering the more difficult content at times when your audience's concentration span is likely to be at its lowest, for example straight after lunch.

Divide the content into your selected headings

Revisit your material and select the information you need to include in each of the selected headings. By filtering this again through your aims you can ensure its relevance.

You may also wish to do another brainstorm at this point and note down the points you feel you should cover under each heading. These can then be pruned down as before. The quote from Kipling on page 4 (what, why, when, how, where and who) can provide a useful checklist to ensure that you have covered all the relevant information you need.

1.9 PREPARING YOUR NOTES

You are now at the point when you need to decide what format your notes should take, and this will depend largely on the type of presentation planned and also your own preferences.

There are certain layouts that are more appropriate for certain types of presentation and you may like to consider trying these out if you have not done so already.

ACTIVITY

If appropriate, think about presentations you have given in the past. How did you prepare your notes? Have you used different approaches? What were the advantages and disadvantages of these?

Compare your experiences and opinions with the notes provided below and then consider what method you will use for your next presentation.

The following are the main methods for preparing your notes.

Full script

There are, in reality, only a few circumstances when a full script will be appropriate. If you are using one, you need to be particularly careful, as your audience can quickly lose interest. This is because no interaction is intended between you and the audience. Your script can also deter you from applying the presentational techniques necessary to sustain interest, for example, body language, movement, use of the natural voice and expressions.

This does not always have to be the case, however. You may feel, for example, far more confident and comfortable with a full script in front of you and as a result better able to concentrate on your performance.

This method, however, is not suitable for situations where a more dynamic or learner-centred approach is required. It won't allow flexibility in approach, content or the pace of learning.

Tips

• Type your script out and use double spacing

• Leave large spaces between paragraphs

• Number your pages clearly and use one side only

• Include prompts for pauses and key words (in case you get lost)

• Rehearse it to ensure it reads well – often the written word is not appropriate when spoken

• Practise and practise until you almost know it off by heart. That way, you will be able to look at the audience (rather than continually at your script) and concentrate more on your presentational techniques. Practising in front of a mirror and with your colleagues will help

• Time your speech – you will alienate your audience if you overrun and they may well feel short-changed if you finish too early. There will normally be other speakers after you and they will also be relying on you to keep to time

• Ask the audience at the beginning to reserve their questions until the end – if you deviate from your script it will be difficult for you to stay on track and also keep to time

- Do leave sufficient time for questions at the end so that the audience has an opportunity to clarify any points they are unclear about or to receive supplementary information

- Think about the types of questions you may be asked and prepare what you are going to say in response. Being 'put on the spot' is one of the biggest fears speakers have but if you have researched your audience beforehand and considered the possible objections or questions you may be asked, you will be well-prepared. If you are asked a question you don't know the answer to, say so and never try to bluff your way out of it.

Cue cards

These can be a useful alternative to a full script or for when you are presenting information in a more informal setting. This method involves your writing out your key headings or learning points on cards (cue or index cards) and using them as prompts to keep you on track.

The advantage of this method is that it allows you to move around and to speak far more naturally than is possible using a full script.

An example of a cue card is provided below:

Good morning! Welcome to course Introduce self Aims/Objectives. (OH1)

Tips
- Avoid the temptation to write out sentences. Condense your content down into key words or prompts

- Include your main questions

- Include the aids and materials at the appropriate time.

Plans or outlines

An outline will normally detail your input (not word for word, however) and also the methods you intend to employ. It can also include your timings and the visual aids you intend to use. An example is provided opposite of the type of layout used.

Presentation title:_____ Visual aids required: _____

Teaching material required *(eg, handouts, flipchart paper, calculator)*

Timings *(start/finish times)*

Time	Presenter's notes	Audience participation	Visual aids	Materials
9.00	Opening greeting. Welcome audience to presentation. Introduce self.			
9.05		Learner to chat with neighbour for five minutes. Introduce to group using flipchart questions as guide	Pre-prepared flipchart on 'how long with job', etc.	
9.20	Explain aims and objectives.		OH1 Aims OH2 Specific objectives.	Give out spare paper and pens if required.

The advantages of this type of format are:

- It is a logical and straightforward format to follow and will enable other presenters to run the same presentation relatively easily in the future or in the event of your being unavailable

- It is particularly useful where you are using a learner-centred approach as it enables you to detail all the activities and materials involved at any one time

- It can be adapted for sessions where there is no formal input and provide you with a simple outline or signposting for the session

- It incorporates audience activities such as group discussions. You can use this column for writing down checklists to ensure that the intended material is covered.

Tips
- Don't write out your presentation in script format, just include the main points you wish to cover

- Use the audience participation column to indicate the activity you will be using and as a checklist of discussion points that you hope will be covered by the group

- Include all the materials and visual aids required and number these. You may also find it helpful to include their title and main points so that you have a good idea of their content without having to refer to them.

Activity in presentations can take many forms. Just as you are using internal reflection as part of working through this text, so, too, you can invite your audience to reflect on things by themselves, assisted by questions. Equally, you may wish to begin your talk with a brainstorm. Alternatively, you may invite people to turn to their neighbours and 'buzz' for several minutes about a topic. You can also pose questions such as: 'How many of you have had to deal with an aggressive colleague?' All of these approaches can help a group to engage with your content in a more 'learner-centred' way, while still ensuring that you can cover your content and achieve your objectives in a limited amount of time.

1.10 SUMMARY

ACTIVITY

Having just worked through this chapter what are the main learning points for you? Jot these down and then consider how you can put them into practice when planning your next presentation.

What aspects of your current practice are you pleased with, and which do you intend to continue with?

Will you require any help in implementing any of your action points? How will you obtain this?

A successful presentation requires careful preparation. If you have followed a proper planning process it will give you increased confidence and help alleviate any anxieties or nerves you may have.

With experience you will develop your expertise and be able to proceed through this stage very quickly. Much of it can become a mental rather than a physical process.

Prior to any type of presentation you will always need to evaluate thoroughly your group's needs and encapsulate these into an overall aim. This can then be broken down into a set of objectives that will provide specific details of your intended outcomes. These outcomes can be written in either behavioural or expressive terms, and need to:

- Be measurable
- Be achievable
- Be relevant
- Include a condition.

In addition to establishing learning needs you will need to research your learners' interests and concerns, your venue, the subject matter, the resources available. Once you have gathered this information you will be well placed to decide on the most appropriate approach to your presentation.

The type of approach you choose will depend on your overall aims and objectives.

Following an interactive approach will greatly assist the effectiveness of your communication with your audience.

The degree to which this is possible will, however, depend on the constraints that you are operating under regarding available resources, number of people and type of learning event.

How you structure your learning event is also of vital importance as this will either enhance or hinder the communication process. There are different ways of preparing your notes but your learning event should always be structured so that it has:

- An introduction, main body and conclusion
- Regular signposting and summaries
- Built in monitoring and reviews
- A logical sequence
- A limited number of main learning points.

CHAPTER 2:
SELECTING AND PREPARING PRESENTATION AIDS

2.1 INTRODUCTION
People remember:

> 10% of what they read
> 20% of what they hear
> 30% of what they see
> But 70% of what they see and hear.

Presentation or visual aids are therefore an extremely useful way of attracting and retaining the attention of your audience.

Most of us are able to concentrate only for a limited amount of time (normally 15-20 minutes) without a change of stimuli or mental break. Relying solely on your voice, no matter how good it is or how skilfully it is used, will not be enough to keep your group's attention for very long. Using visual aids can help, therefore, to maintain or rekindle concentration and so lengthen their capacity to learn effectively. Visual aids can help clarify complex or abstract information or ideas that are simply too difficult to describe or mentally absorb without putting them onto paper.

They also help aid the memory. Remember the adage 'I hear and I forget, I see and I remember?'

Finally, visual aids can enhance your group's enjoyment of your presentation, most of us being naturally drawn to pictorial or written images.

Appropriate and timely use of presentation aids
Aids are not always necessary. You may, for example, choose not to use them where there is no formalised content or knowledge element, or where you are communicating simple ideas or information that can be easily stated verbally.

Pre-preparing slides or boards

Whether or not you should use pre-prepared aids really depends on the type of presentation you are using. For a conference or formal business presentation, for example, where it is critical that your visual aids look polished, they should be professionally prepared wherever possible.

The advantages of having pre-prepared aids are:

- They look very professional
- You can give full attention to your presentation
- You will not omit any important learning points
- They can keep you on track
- They take up less time in the presentation than writing points down as you talk.
- They are usually more legible and easier to read than writing on a board yourself.

There are, however, certain drawbacks:

- They suggest a prescriptive approach
- You will not be able to add to or adapt the material
- The words you use are not necessarily those of your audience.

In situations where you are using an interactive approach you will be looking for a high degree of learner involvement, so it is likely that you will prefer to build up much of your material in conjunction with the learners. This will also enable you to use the learners' own language.

In reality, presenters often use both approaches together, with the pre-prepared material being used when they are delivering input.

Finally, visual aids will not automatically assist the learning process. When handled badly, they can prove to be a hindrance rather than a help. They will never substitute for poor presentational skills or inadequate planning.

Difficulties can often arise when the presenter tries to use more aids than they or the audience can cope with. But above all, you need to be competent and confident with the visual aids you use, and to have practised using them beforehand in tandem with your script.

2.2 USE OF BOARDS

There are three main types of boards that you can use:
> The blackboard
> The whiteboard
> The flipchart.

The blackboard

This is the visual aid that is mostly associated with teaching and the traditional 'chalk and talk' method. Some blackboards include a roll-down mechanism to enable you to conceal previously prepared work or to keep earlier work for later reference. Dust-free chalk is produced nowadays, which alleviates much of the mess previously associated with blackboards.

Despite the advances just mentioned, there is still a general reluctance by presenters to use this type of board because of its associations with a classroom setting. It certainly does not look very professional and most presenters, given the choice, would opt for the whiteboard.

The whiteboard

The whiteboard, with its white glossy finish, offers a much more professional and attractive looking visual aid than the blackboard. It also often doubles up as a magnetic board if free-mounted and enables pre-prepared work to be concealed until required.

There are certain disadvantages, however. Whiteboards require the use of dry marker pens, and if there are other

35

visual aids around it is very easy for the wrong type of pen to be used. Where this happens, the board needs to be cleaned with special remover and this can be a very messy process. In addition, unlike the roll-down blackboards, you are very limited for space and therefore whiteboards are not suitable for situations in which you need to be able to refer back to earlier notes.

The flipchart

The flipchart is a versatile and popular visual aid consisting of a portable easel and a pad of A2-size paper. It can be moved to any situation required, and previously prepared work can simply be flipped over and revealed as necessary. The sheets are also easily detachable and can be used for groupwork. These can then be remounted onto the easel or attached to the wall.

A drawback with the flipchart is that it can be rather cumbersome when you are searching for previous charts or are flipping the sheets back and forth.

ACTIVITY

In what circumstances would you use any or all of the above aids?

You may have found all three boards particulary useful for:

- Developing an idea
- Presenting information step by step
- Recording discussion points or feedback
- Emphasising key words
- Giving an instruction or message.

The flipchart is the most suitable board for recording information you may wish to keep or refer back to later in your presentation. The sheets can also be used for displaying information on the walls. In addition, where a large amount of information is being covered, the flipchart is an easier medium to work with than the other two boards, which require regular cleaning. With the whiteboard and blackboard, you can also find yourself running out of room at an inappropriate moment and having to erase material that you would rather have retained.

Tips

- Write legibly and neatly

- Ensure you have a supply of pens (including spares) and that they work. There is nothing more frustrating for you or your audience than trying to write with pens that are running out

- Ensure you have sufficient flipchart paper

- Use blue or black pens for text. These are strong colours and therefore easy to see from a distance – reserve other colours such as red and green for underlining, tabulations, and so on

- Be consistent in the style you use. This is a point common to all visual aids

- Ensure your writing can be seen, and leave sufficient space between lines. (Practise this if you aren't sure. Letters need to be about three inches high)

- Use capitals. (These are easier to read than your own handwriting)

- Put your pen or chalk down when you have finished writing. (This will stop you playing with it and distracting your group)

- Use a fresh flipchart for new information

- Rub out any unrelated information

- Keep the board surfaces clean. (Ensure you have a board rubber available)

- Use two boards – one for pre-prepared work and the other for recording key points during the event

- Plan your usage beforehand. You can pre-prepare both your boards and charts. This will give you the time to ensure they look really professional. Alternatively, you can prepare the content lightly on the boards and then simply trace the material as required. This will provide you with very effective prompts or cues when you are trying to draw a complicated diagram (or straight lines)

- Do not put too much information onto one board or page. Avoid writing out whole sentences – stick to key words and give your learners sufficient time to read each chart before moving on to the next

- Do not talk while you are writing. This will reduce the risk of your talking with your back to the learner.

ACTIVITY

How would you rate your existing skills when using boards – on a scale of 1-10? What are some of the things you want to work on especially when you (next) give a presentation? Is there anyone who could help you do this, such as by being a 'practice audience' or by giving feedback at the event itself?

What will you do differently, more or less as a result of reading this section? What will you do as you have always done because you are now more confident that it helps to make communication more effective?

2.3 THE OVERHEAD PROJECTOR

The overhead projector is another popular visual aid and can be used with either pre-prepared or blank acetates (also known as foils or transparencies). Acetates can be produced professionally and projected on to a screen or wall. As there is usually a focus on the projector, it is possible to project either a small or large image. The projector can therefore be used with larger audiences than boards can be used with.

The room does not need to be darkened and you can face your learner as you write on or refer to the acetate. You do, however, need to ensure that the projector arm is not blocking any of your audience's view of the screen. Check that it is situated in the right position for you to operate it easily. (Which side you have it on will normally depend on whether you are right-or left-handed.)

ACTIVITY

Think about your own experience of overhead projectors, either as a presenter or as a member of an audience. In what ways did it enhance the quality and effectiveness of your communication with the audience? In what ways might your use of an overhead projector have hindered the audience's learning? Are there circumstances in which you would not use an overhead projector and, if so, why? When do you think it is especially helpful, and why?

You may previously have used an overhead projector for:

- *Speaking at a conference* – acetates are easy to transport and when produced professionally look much more professional than boards

- *Presenting information and concepts*

- *Building up ideas* – either using a blank acetate or overlay sheets. Overlay sheets enable you to build up points by using one acetate with basic information on it and then overlaying additional foils with supplementary material.

Tips
- Write legibly, using key points rather than sentences. (See previous tips for boards. Again be consistent in the style you use)

- Do not obscure the screen. This is very easy to do, particularly when you are writing on an acetate. Try to keep to the side of the projector and regulary check to ensure that the content is not obscured by your shadow

- Ensure all of the acetate can be seen. It is too easy to assume that because *you* can see all of the acetate, your learners can. You need to check that they have a complete view of each acetate you show

- Check you have a spare bulb, blank foils and projector pens. With some projectors you can switch over to a secondary bulb system. You should always check that your spare bulb is working and know how to replace it should one burn out during your presentation

- As with the boards, you also need to check that your pens have not run dry. (If you are preparing your own acetates use permanent pens whenever possible as the water-based pens do smudge)

- Ensure the screen and lens surfaces are clean. This will help the image to be as clear as possible

- Point to the acetate rather than to the screen. This will stop you from turning your back on your learners. You may wish to use a pointer or alternatively a pencil placed on the acetate and pointed at the relevant part of the acetate

- Switch off the projector after each acetate. The noise of the projector and the bright light shining onto the screen can be very distracting for learners. The projector can also get very hot although there will normally be a cooling fan mechanism to prevent the projector from overheating

- Where you have a number of key points, show only the relevant part. This will help your audience to focus on a particular point. Use a piece of paper underneath the acetate (that way it won't slip off) and slowly reveal your points as required

- Use strong colours, for example, blue and black for words

- Practise using the projector beforehand. Each projector will be slightly different and if you practise beforehand you can ensure your screen is in the right position and that your acetates are in focus

- Number your acetates and do not have too many. Ensure there is a good reason for every acetate you use and that you restrict the number, as your group will lose interest if they are used to excess

- Place the acetates in order in an upside down position beside the projector when you have finished with them, so that they are ready to be used again if necessary

- Place acetates in protective sleeves. This will ensure they remain dust-free. Some sleeves include side sleeves and many presenters use these for jotting down key words

- Tilt the screen forward to prevent keystoning. Keystoning is when you have a picture that is narrower at the bottom than at the top and parts of the image are out of focus.

ACTIVITY

Rate your existing skills in using a projector on a scale of 1-10. How can you improve your competence in this area?

2.4 VIDEO

The video can be a highly effective resource. It will add a professional touch to your presentation and can be entertaining. In addition, learners will normally find it easy to concentrate when watching a film (remember they will be using two senses – hearing and seeing). It is therefore very useful at particular times of the day when attention may be flagging, for example, following lunch or after a lecture.

There are a great number of training films on the market (either to buy or lend), covering a range of topics. These come in a number of different video formats but the most popular is VHS.

Before you decide to include a video in your presentation, however, there are certain considerations you should bear in mind:

- The film may not be completely relevant or consistent with your proposed content

Unless you have produced the video yourself, it is highly unlikely that all of its contents will be appropriate or consistent with your aims, and it may be difficult to show only specific parts of the film.

- The humour may detract from the learning content

Many films use famous actors and a humorous approach, and this can result in learners remembering the film for its entertainment value rather than for the learning content.

- Some films are poorly made

It is easy to assume that a professionally made film is going to be well made. This may not be the case, however, so you need to check through the video very carefully before you decide to use it.

- The film may be out of date – again this needs to be checked beforehand

Videos can be particularly useful for:

- Demonstrating communication processes, behaviour and events – for example, different attitudes, approaches and outcomes

- Presenting scenarios or a case study

- Providing a conceptual framework or helping learners to visualise a particular setting or series of events

- Summarising a large topic

- Capturing the audience's interest – for example, 'trigger videos' are designed to provoke a response from the audience.

Tips
- Always include an introduction and summary of the learning points

- You need to treat showing the video as if you were running an entirely separate session. In other words, explain where the film fits in in relation to your aims and objectives and provide a brief resumé of its content and title. ('Tell them what you're going to tell them')

A post-film discussion or review can be used to draw out key learning points and relate them to the audience's own situation and experiences.

In a large group, this can be achieved by inviting people to spend a few minutes talking to the person next to them, perhaps focused by a question posed by you. You might then ask them to brainstorm in response to another question, such as: 'What did you feel when watching that scene?'

Finish with a brief summary. ('Tell them what you've told them'.)

- Check that your equipment is working and that your tape is wound back to the appropriate point

- Where possible, play only those parts of the film that are relevant. Where there are a number of topics or points covered in the film you may decide to play it in short clips. This will give the group time before moving onto the next topic.

Using the video counter will help you to locate quickly the sections you require.

- Check that each group member is able to see the video screen or TV monitor

- Invite people to move if necessary. You may also need to darken the room to achieve a clearer picture

- Familiarise yourself thoroughly with the film content prior to using it in the learning event

- You may find it useful to have a brief summary of its contents in your notes

- Remain present when the film is being shown – you need to see what sort of reaction the video is having on your audience and to prepare for any subsequent questions or confusion

- Forewarn them of what is to follow the video – this will help them to concentrate and prepare for what follows. It will also deter them from just viewing the film for its entertainment value.

2.5 AUDIO TAPES

Audio tapes are more often seen as a distance learning resource but they can also be used to good effect in a face-to-face situation. You need to ensure that your environment is suitably quiet, however, otherwise your audience will find it very difficult to concentrate.

Audio tapes are often used for:

- Music
- Sound effects
- Dramatisation of an event
- Setting the scene
- Recitals and quotes
- Short lectures by subject matter experts
- Recording group discussions and role-plays.

Tips
- Check your audio equipment beforehand

- Check that there are power points nearby

- Pre-set the volume and ensure the tape is wound back to the appropriate point

- Ensure usage relates to overall aims and objectives and that this is explained to learners beforehand

- Introduce and summarise the contents (see tips for using videos).

Use group discussion to process contents where appropriate.

2.6 SLIDES

ACTIVITY

What effect does the use of professional slides have on you as an audience member? Under what circumstances do they help the communication process? How might they diminish effective communication between you and the presenter?

The 35mm slide projector, like the overhead projector, can be used with either a wall or a screen. It is a very popular medium and the slides can be produced using a wide variety of colours and to a very high professional standard. The range of material they can cover is extensive, including photographs, diagrams, charts and logos. Slides can, however, be costly and take time to prepare. You need to ensure, therefore, that you have sufficient time to produce them and that they do not contain information that is likely to become out of date quickly .

To achieve a clear image, you really need to darken the room and this can make it more difficult for you to remain in contact with your audience.

Tips

- *Check your equipment thoroughly* – ensure that the power cable will reach the socket and that you are completely confident operating the equipment

- *Check the lighting arrangements* – you may wish to nominate someone beforehand to switch the lights on and off for you. You also need to ensure that you will be able to read your presentation notes when the lights are off

- *Insert slides in every other slot of the carousel* – this enables you to remove one slide and leave the screen blank while you continue with your presentation. It also prevents the audience from becoming distracted from what you are saying. You may consider substituting the blank screen with your company logo and this is perfectly acceptable

- *Keep to the side of the screen* – this will prevent you from obscuring your group's view and casting your own shadow onto the screen

It is also very important that you check continuously that your notes or audio presentation correspond to the slide being shown.

Showing the wrong slide can have hilarious consequences and make it difficult for you to regain both your own composure and your audience's concentration. If your slides are out of order it will also take some time to sort them out and so it is vital that these are thoroughly checked beforehand.

- When transporting slides, place them in a carousel. This will keep them in the right order as well as dust-free

- Number your slides – both in your notes and on the slide itself

- Where possible, use a hand remote control to operate the slides. This will enable you to be mobile and operate the equipment from wherever you choose

- Limit your content to key words, use capitals and ensure the words can be seen (see notes on use of boards).

ACTIVITY

Again, rate your existing competence and assess whether there are any areas in which you can improve. Are there any tips you can add to the checklist?

2.7 HANDOUTS

When in doubt, hand out

(Anon)

ACTIVITY

What message do you think that this saying conveys when you think about your own experience as a presenter? In what ways can handouts help or hinder the quality of communication and learning during a presentation? What tips would you give yourself, as a future presenter?

Providing handouts can be of great value for your audience. For example, they avoid the necessity of copious note-taking, which can be very distracting and gives your audience little time to analyse what is being said.

However, many people genuinely find note-taking he.
and prefer to have notes in their own words.

Handouts should usually be given out at the end of your
session so that they do not become a distraction from your
talk. However, you may sometimes choose to distribute
them at the outset, particularly where you are covering a lot
of new material. This will then enable the group to use the
handout as a working document and to add their own
supplementary notes as required.

Remember to inform your audience at the start of the
presentation that there will be handouts at the end as well,
and what and how much information will be contained on
them.

Handouts also provide a means for ensuring that an
accurate account of the main learning points is recorded for
the audience to read and to take away after the presentation.
They can also look attractive and professional. It is possible
nowadays to produce handouts to a very high standard with
the aid of word-processing and desk-top publishing
packages.

ACTIVITY

Think about the content you might use in a presentation. In what ways might your effective communication of that content be assisted by the use of handouts? What other visual aids would you want to enlist?

What to include

What you do not want to include is a full resumé of your
presentation, as the longer the handout the less likely it will
be read.

A summary of the main points covered is probably of the
greatest value. Use of side headings and checklists will help
the audience to grasp the content quickly. The use of
cartoons, will further help to attract attention and illustrate
the points you are making.

If you do decide to distribute the handout prior to, or

during, the presentation, a wide margin at the side of the page will provide space for the learner to expand on the points raised.

2.8 SETTING UP THE ROOM

We have already mentioned the importance of being well-prepared, and having a suitable and well-organised learning environment is an important part of this process.

You may not always have a choice as to the location of your presentation and there may be problems with it that are beyond your control. However, by familiarising yourself with it beforehand you will put yourself in a much better position for dealing with problems as they arise.

Another important part of your preparations should be the completion of a checklist of all the materials required in your presentation. This will ensure that you don't forget anything, and prevent any last minute panic.

ACTIVITY

Think about situations where the learning environment had a positive or negative effect on the effectiveness of a presentation and the presenter. What learning points can you draw from this experience?

You may have included some of the following:

- *Size of room* – is it appropriate for the size of the group and the approach you have chosen?

Too small a room will make it very uncomfortable for the learners, who will find it increasingly difficult to concentrate. Too large a room may make them self-conscious.

It is suggested that you remove any spare chairs once all the learners have arrived.

- *Room temperature* – if the room lacks ventilation and is hot and stuffy, your group will get increasingly drowsy and listless. Alternatively, if it is too cold, they will become tense and uncomfortable. Often the choice will be a noisy but hot room, or a quiet and cool room

If the event includes a refreshment break this is a very useful time to open the windows and let in some fresh air.

- *Lighting* – test out the lighting beforehand to see which are the most appropriate lighting arrangements. In particular, you need to ensure that the lights don't make it difficult to see the visual aids

- *Seating arrangements* – This will depend largely on the size of the group and the type of approach to be used. If you are giving a formal presentation with visual aids, for example, you may prefer a u-shape or classroom layout with a table at the top. This will enable your group to make notes and see any visual aids.

For a more informal learning method, such as a presentation involving group discussion, you may prefer a circle layout with you sitting as part of the group.

Alternatively, you may prefer the learners to sit together in groups to facilitate discussion of key points in your presentation. You need to ensure, however, that no learners have their backs to you or have to twist round to see you or the visual aid.

- *Equipment* – refer to your checklist for the equipment you will be using. This needs to be set up well in advance of the presentation and thoroughly checked (see earlier notes). You also need to ensure that there are no cables trailing where people can trip over them

If you are using a microphone, again practise using this beforehand.

- *Domestic and safety arrangements* – these should be covered at the beginning of the session unless you know that they have been covered already

- *Likely distractions* – as mentioned previously, if you know about these beforehand you are better placed to deal with them.

2.9 SUMMARY

ACTIVITY

Reflect back on this chapter. What has been most useful for you? What do you want to think about more, or do differently when you next do a presentation? Which visual aids are you most/least confident about using?

What support or practice do you require in order to build your repertoire of skills and for working with different types of groups in different kinds of circumstances?

Although not always necessary, visual aids can be a valuable asset in your presentation. They can:

- Clarify difficult or complex concepts
- Aid retention
- Add to the overall enjoyment of the presentation.

There are a number of visual aids available and your choice will depend on factors including:

- The resources that you have at your disposal
- Their cost
- Time available for preparation
- Size of group
- The approach
- Your own and others' preferences
- The learning environment.

Tips

- Do not use too many aids in a single presentation
- Limit the number of slides you use
- Check your equipment thoroughly beforehand
- Keep to the side of the aid
- Do not crowd your slides or charts with too much information
- Write legibly and neatly
- Allow your audience time to read each slide/board
- Position your aids where your audience can see them
- Prepare a checklist
- Check out the environment beforehand – including any likely distractions.

Most of us have one type of visual aid that we feel particularly comfortable with and tend to use a lot. However you will increase your own versatility as a presenter if you develop your competence across the full range of visual aids, and you may wish to include this as an objective to achieve after working through this Handbook.

CHAPTER 3:
DELIVERING YOUR PRESENTATION

3.1 INTRODUCTION

ACTIVITY

Think about your own style and personality. When do you feel confident and most effective as a communicator? What skills and qualities do you use in situations where you trust that you are relating well to your audience and helping them to learn effectively?

Whether you are speaking at a conference in front of 100 people or presenting to a group of colleagues, *how* you deliver your presentation will depend on your own personality and individual style. Remember the saying: 'Know thyself.'

You should develop a presentational style that reflects your own personality. We have all at some time or another compared our abilities with those of somebody we admire. If you are tempted to emulate someone else, you will not be behaving naturally and this will immediately be picked up by your audience. So you need to concentrate on *yourself* – what is good about your own presentation style and those aspects that perhaps you need to change.

Notwithstanding these comments, you may find other presenters helpful in showing you some techniques and tips, but it remains essential that the style you use is your very own.

This chapter will be looking at the main factors that will contribute to your success as a presenter and how you can improve your techniques in each of these areas.

3.2 EFFECTIVE COMMUNICATION SKILLS

For every type of presentation your own delivery skills need to be first class in order to promote an effective exchange of information and ideas with your learners.

Where you are running a formal presentation or speaking at a conference, you may view yourself as a performer but in every situation you are a critical resource – one that can have a positive or negative impact on the communication process.

One way of helping you to develop your existing skills is to ask a trusted friend or colleague to sit in on one of your presentations and evaluate your performance.

ACTIVITY

Talk with someone who is familiar with your style and learn more about how and why you come across effectively or not. Are there particular circumstances you need to be alert to?

The following questions will help you to extend this conversation.

1. **Using a scale of 1-10 how confident do you feel when you are making a presentation? How do you deal with any nerves and how effective are the methods you use?**

2. **How effectively do you use your voice and body language?**

3. **On a scale of 1-10 how happy are you with your presentation style?**

4. **What are your particular strengths?**

5. **Which aspects of your performance do you need to work on? How will you do this?**

6. **If there were two or three things you would particularly like feedback on when you next make a presentation, what would they be, and why? What would you like to work on with regard to these?**

There are a number of different aspects to consider when analysing your presentational style and these are covered below.

Body language

Even when you are standing on a rostrum in front of a large audience and reading from a script, it is important to consider your use of body language.

If you do not, your presentation can lack vitality and enthusiasm and your voice will lose its natural animation.

Eighty per cent of the messages we convey to people are non-verbal. If you think about it, we use gestures in normal conversation without even thinking about it. Your body language will help your audience to understand what you are saying and, in addition, will help you use your voice more expressively.

Every one of us has our own special mannerisms and facial expressions and you will subconsciously know what type of gestures to use when you speak. So you will be using an established language that your learner automatically understands – therein lies a danger, as, if you are *not* being sincere, your words will be saying one thing and your body language another.

Where you have a larger audience your body language may have to be more pronounced to ensure that everyone is able to see you. This does not mean you have to over-dramatise your actions but it may involve your having to operate at a more conscious level than usual.

Using body language consciously can be difficult if you are also to be as natural as possible. If you feel this is going to be difficult for you, practise in front of a mirror or preferably using a video recorder.

Until you gain confidence try not distract the learner by adopting repetitive mannerisms or habits, as these can quickly begin to irritate or annoy. Typical habits include:

• Swaying from one foot to the other
• Jingling change in pockets
• Fiddling with pieces of chalk, pointers, pens
• Exaggerated or meaningless gestures
• Repetitive use of a word or phrase
• Avoidance of eye-contact
• Putting hands in pockets or behind backs
• Wearing jewellery that 'jangles'.

Another problem experienced by new presenters is what to do with their hands. While standing, the most natural thing is to have your hands hanging relaxed by your side. When you are sitting, you may prefer to have them resting lightly on your knees or on the desk. What you should avoid is:

• Clasping them together either to the front or back
• Keeping hands in pockets
• The 'fig-leaf' position.

Finally, when talking about body language, it is easy just to concentrate on arms, feet and legs, but your face is also very important. In our everyday conversations, our facial expressions are critical to the communication process, which is why so many of us do not like talking on the telephone. So use your face to communicate your meaning – look at your learners and *smile!*

Standing or sitting

In informal presentations, particularly where you wish 'control' to be passed to the learner (such as during a group discussion), sitting down will help to promote interaction.

In most other situations, however, standing up will almost certainly improve your presentation techniques. Many presenters worry, however, that standing up is indicative of a formal approach, but this is not necessarily the case. Certainly it looks professional but equally it can look very informal, particularly where you move among the group or towards them at particular points. You can always sit down for group discussions or when someone is talking and then when you subsequently stand up you will be signalling to your group that you need to move on.

Whichever stance you prefer, your position may well be dictated by the circumstances of your presentation, your visual aids and also the type of notes that you are using. Where you are using a microphone that does not have an extension lead or is not the type that clips on to your clothes, you will have little choice but to remain in one spot. Having a lectern will also discourage you from moving about, although you could always move to the side or in front of it if you wished to get closer to your audience. Cue cards, on the other hand, will give you freedom to move about without losing track of where you are in the presentation.

If you have opted for a desk, standing behind it can make you feel more confident and in control but will, in addition, suggest to your audience that you will be adopting a more formal approach and relationship. This can intimidate some learners who may feel you are less approachable, and they may be less willing to speak out.

ACTIVITY

To demonstrate the impact body language has on the voice try describing a thunderstorm without using any gestures. Now repeat this using body language and see what effect it has on your voice pattern.

You have probably found that your pace, pitch and volume are more varied the second time round and that you have managed to convey far more about what a storm entails.

Another useful exercise to try is to attempt to describe a spiral staircase without using your hands – it is a great deal more difficult for you to describe and for the learner to understand.

Being nervous about presenting can often inhibit your ability to use body language and you may feel completely rooted to the spot.

If you are in a classroom-type setting, you may be used to sitting down and this can again interfere with your voice pattern and body language.

Voice

There are four main aspects to consider in relation to your voice:

1. Projection

Where you have a large group and don't have a microphone available, you need to be able to project your voice so that your group can hear you. This doesn't mean that you should shout – increasing your volume this way will only make you hoarse and will distort the sound.

In order to project your voice you need to:

• Keep your head up
• Speak slightly more slowly than in normal speech
• Open your mouth slightly wider
• Speak as clearly as possible.

This technique is used most effectively by stage actors and will ensure you will be heard even in a very large room. Where you have a particularly soft voice it is a good idea to practise this with a colleague beforehand.

Varying your volume will also maintain interest, convey meaning and give further emphasis to certain parts of your presentation.

2. Pace

The tendency for most of us when we are nervous is to talk too quickly. Even if you are confident, this can be a problem as learners may not be familiar with your speech patterns or accent.

You need to ensure, therefore, that you are speaking slightly more slowly than you would normally, particularly if you have a strong accent.

3. Pauses

The use of the pause is a very effective way of renewing or maintaining your group's interest. It will create an atmosphere of expectation, with your audience sitting in a kind of suspense until you re-commence your presentation. You can allow a period of silence to go on for longer than you may initially think. You can use this technique when you need to:

- Regain their interest
- Write on visual aids
- Move onto another part of your presentation
- Give the learner time to digest the previous point
- Emphasise the importance of what you have just said or are about to say
- Encourage the learners to respond to a question or discuss a topic.

If you have a tendency to talk quickly you may wish to annotate your notes with instructions on when to pause or to leave large gaps between points so that you automatically slow down at regular intervals.

Varying your pace will also add meaning and emphasis to what you are saying.

Have you ever noticed how great orators use timing for effect? The famous words used by Winston Churchill illustrates this perfectly:

Never in the field of human endeavour
has so much been owed
by so many
to so few

You may not wish to be this dramatic, but at a conference, for example, you may wish to pay particular attention to the wording and timing of your introduction and conclusion. These are the times when an audience's concentration level will be greatest.

4. Pitch
Most of us will vary our pitch when speaking normally or when we are relaxed and confident. Anxiety can, however, result in a monotone voice that lacks animation or variety of pitch. There is no doubt that a monotone voice is very hard on the hearing and this will make it difficult for the listener to maintain concentration.

Eye contact

Eye contact with your group is vital if you are to establish and maintain a relationship with its members. Avoiding eye contact may suggest that you are nervous, bored or possibly being insincere.

Eye contact has a number of functions. It:
• Provides you with feedback as to how your learners are reacting to what is being said
• Gains and holds attention
• Establishes and builds rapport
• Involves the listener
• Makes your presentation more personal.

Where you have a small group, establish eye contact with each member but avoid making them feel uncomfortable by focusing on them for too long.

If the group is too large for you to look at each person individually, then you need to make eye contact with different individuals in different parts of the room.

What you should try to avoid is:

- Looking above people's heads
- Looking at the same person all of the time (it can be particularly tempting, for example, to fix on a friendly face when you are unsure of your reception)
- Sweeping the room without actually establishing eye contact with anyone
- Ignoring one section of the audience or room (this can be easily done and will make the members feel excluded from the experience).

When asked a question the general rule is that you give the asker two-thirds of the eye contact and the remaining one-third to the rest of the group. This will acknowledge the special interest shown by the questioner without excluding everyone else.

Questions and answers

Whatever your type of presentation, at some point you will wish to give your group the chance to ask for further clarification, proffer an alternative view, or respond to what you have said.

When you are running a formal presentation you will probably prefer to take questions at the end, as this will enable you to remain within time and stay on track. The drawback of this method is that your learners won't have the opportunity to seek help until the end of the presentation, and this can interfere with the learning process, particularly where there is a gradual build-up of ideas.

This is why other learner-centred methods, such as brainstorming, pairs discussion and individual reflection, can be useful.

The best way of inviting questions at the end of a presentation is to ask: '*What* questions do you have?' rather than '*Does* anyone have any questions?' Assuming there will be questions will encourage your audience to ask them.

If you have done your preparation, you will probably have anticipated many of the questions and have the answers at your fingertips. If you do not know the answer, say so. You risk losing credibility if you try to bluff your way through. Equally, do not attempt to answer any question that you do not fully understand. Ask the person to repeat it for you or paraphrase it before checking it back with the questioner.

In a more informal setting you will probably invite full participation by the learner at every stage of your presentation and will wish to ask questions yourself to:

- Check understanding
- Invite participation and interaction
- Develop ideas and concepts
- Review a particular topic or area
- Invite alternative viewpoints and opinions.

You need to prepare your main questions beforehand and incorporate these within your presentation notes. Use open rather than closed questions such as, how, why and what, as these will require more of a response than a simple yes or no.

ACTIVITY

Imagine yourself in front of a large group. In your mind's eye, experience your body language and your use of eye contact. Where can you imagine that you might have difficulties? How might you unintentionally alienate your group? What kinds of messages do you want to incorporate at different stages in your notes?

Factors to avoid

There are a number of ways that you might unintentionally embarrass or alienate your audience. These include:

- *Using bad language* – in certain situations, such as at an after dinner speech you may feel that using expletives is appropriate. If you have sufficiently researched your audience you could well be right. However, you will always run the risk of causing offence to at least a few members of your audience. Using bad language is not professional or the way to build rapport with your audience.

- *Making discriminatory remarks* – as with bad language will almost certainly insult some of your learners if yc make remarks against certain sectors of society.

- *Using humour* – humour is a very effective way of building rapport and holding attention.

Few people are naturally funny, however, and there is nothing more embarrassing than someone telling a joke badly. People also laugh at different things, so don't expect everyone to appreciate your particular brand of humour. If you are in any doubt about using humour – then don't.

- *Talking at an inappropriate level* – this is where your previous research comes in useful. You do not wish to insult your group by assuming no prior knowledge, while at the same time you do not want to confuse them by using technical jargon they do not understand.

Check your audience's understanding of technical terms at the beginning of the presentation through questioning or by including a brief explanation of the terminology you will be using.

- *Failing to relate the content to the group's own situation* – where practical, invite group members to share their experiences and thoughts in small group settings. In formal presentations use analogies or practical examples to illustrate the points you are making. Try to use ones that your audience will be likely to have encountered.

Anecdotes are very useful for entertainment value and for illustrating a particular point. Again these need to be well-researched and relevent to the overall content or point you are discussing.

- *Adopting an inappropriate style* – your language, dress and manner should all be appropriate for the people you will be working with.

Where dress is concerned, there are two schools of thought. Some people believe you should match your group's style, while others feel that business or smart dress is always more appropriate.

3.3 STARTING YOUR PRESENTATION

People's attention span during a presentation will fluctuate to varying degrees and this will depend on a number of different factors. If the presentation includes a change in stimuli at regular intervals your audience will find it easier to concentrate for longer periods. Your own presentation skills will also be an important influence.

Other contributing factors often not considered are the personal circumstances and experiences of your group. An individual could, for example, have a personal problem that will affect his/her ability to concentrate. Alternatively, someone may not find the approach you are taking is compatible with his/her own preferred learning style, or that the subject matter is of particular relevance.

At the beginning of the presentation, however, most learners will not have any preconceived views about the effectiveness of your presentation

They will most likely be hoping and expecting to have a positive learning experience.

It is down to you, therefore, to make the most of their open-mindedness by convincing them that it is worth their while to listen.

The value of an introduction

The introduction is the most important part of the presentation in that the learners' concentration levels will be at their highest. They will be at their freshest and will be waiting for you to convince them that your presentation will be of interest to them. If you fail to grab their attention at this stage, it will be very difficult to regain it later on.

Have you noticed how often delegates at a conference will often stay to hear the introduction of a speech and then get up and leave?

Your own group members may not be able physically to remove themselves from the room but if they are convinced the presentation is not for them, mentally they will be through the door before you know it.

Likewise, at the end of a presentation your learners will increase their concentration level as they wait for the signals to tell them it is time to leave. This is an opportunity, therefore, to consolidate further what you have said by summarising the key learning points of the presentation.

ACTIVITY

Think of a recent presentation you either attended or delivered. How were the introduction and conclusion handled? How did these assist or hinder the learning process for you?

Any presentation, be it an after dinner speech or a 10-minute lecture, should have a beginning, a middle and an end.

This is the first part of the phrase:

Tell them what you're going to tell them.
Tell them.
Tell them what you've told them.

The main body is the middle part, and the last the conclusion.

The introduction therefore needs to:
• Describe the aim and objectives
• Set the scene – your group members will want to know what is going to happen, what will be expected of them and what they can expect from you
• Introduce you (and, where it is an interactive session, the group members themselves).

You may also wish to ask the group members to consider their own objectives at this stage. Only ask for these, however, if you are prepared to adapt your material accordingly.

• Gain the group's attention

There are a number of ways that you can generate initial interest in your presentation. You can, for example, simply relate the benefits to the group members when discussing the aims and objectives.

Alternatively, you can use some sort of stimuli to attract their attention.

You might begin a talk on assertiveness, for example, by acting out a loud argument between a shopkeeper and a customer. The object of the exercise would be to demonstrate the difference between aggressive and assertive behaviour.

Ice-breakers have a different role to play in that they can help to create a more relaxed atmosphere at the beginning of your presentation.

This is particulary important where time is limited.

There are a number of ice-breaker exercises available on the market but it is also very easy for you to make one up yourself. The main criteria for an ice-breaker are as follows:

- It needs to be quick. Normally there is little teaching content in the exercise and time will be limited so it shouldn't last for more than 5-10 minutes

- It needs to be fun. You want to relax your group and help them get to know each other

- It needs to be easy to understand

- It needs to be appropriate.

An example of an ice-breaker at a presentation on communication within an organisation is a 'grapevine' exercise.

This involves writing a longish sentence out on a piece of paper and allowing one person to look at it for a few seconds. He/she then has to repeat the sentence verbally to another group member *once* only. The process is repeated until the message has passed round all members of the group. The last person to receive the message then repeats it out loud and this is compared with the original sentence.

The results are normally hilarious and the exercise is a good way of making everyone feel relaxed, while showing the way that information is gradually distorted as it passes from one person to another.

3.4 THE AWKWARD CUSTOMER

However much you research your audience you will at some time or another find yourself faced with a hostile group member.

Burying your head in the sand or ignoring the situation will only compound the problem. You need to address any difficulties straight away to avoid the situation worsening or others losing confidence in you, too.

ACTIVITY

Imagine that you are giving a presentation. You feel confident that you are communicating effectively until one of the group begins to interrupt you continually in a hostile manner and dispute what you are saying. At first you are pleased to be challenged but then it becomes increasingly clear that the person is trying to sabotage your presentation. Whispered asides are being made to the individual's neighbour who is clearly feeling embarrassed and uncomfortable. The rest of the group members are also becoming distracted and you feel that if you don't do something soon your credibility and the presentation will be badly affected.

How would you feel? What would you, ideally, like to do? What would you probably do? What factors would influence how you would actually respond? What experience of this kind of situation can you draw upon? What kinds of strategies have worked well and what have worked less well?

Make a list of key learning points from this reflection.

When you have an 'awkward customer' there are a number of techniques you can apply:

- Direct a specific question to the person to make it clear you want him/her to participate.

This technique is useful where you have a group member who is indicating through his/her body language, lack of interest in what you are saying. It will give you the opportunity to encourage a positive contribution as well as to get some idea if there is a problem. It is also a non-confrontational way of letting the person know that you have noticed the lack of attention and wish for some participation.

- Take the person aside at a suitable break and ask if there are any problems

This will take the person out of the group setting and avoid others from getting involved. Without an audience the person may also be less confrontational and you may find that there is an understandable explanation for the behaviour which can easily be remedied.

Alternatively, if you have to, do not be afraid to point out that you have certain requirements in terms of behaviour, and explain the negative impact that this person's behaviour is having on the group as a whole.

- Ask the person to leave

This is the last resort but if your 'awkward customer' doesn't want to be there, he/she will get nothing from the experience and is also likely to prevent everyone else from deriving any benefit.

- Invite the person to share his/her opinions with the rest of the group, or pause

This can be used when a learner persists in making casual asides to a neighbour. It is again non-confrontational but will let the person know you are aware that he/she is causing a distraction.

- Ask the person to help the other learners

This is an effective technique for dealing with someone who is constantly taking over the discussion and not allowing others to speak.

Compliment such people on their obvious knowledge of the topic then suggest that as they are already very familiar with this area, they help you facilitate any further group activities and encourage others to answer the majority of the questions.

- Invite the group to respond to a confrontational reply

Avoiding a one-to-one confrontation is critical, as engaging in a battle of words or putting a person down is not only unprofessional, but will also alienate the rest of the group.

You should, therefore, let the rest of the group sort out the situation themselves by asking *them* to respond to a negative or confrontational view.

This is a highly effective technique as normally the difficult member will bow to peer pressure and readjust his/her behaviour accordingly.

It is to be hoped that you will not be required to use these tactics very often but you should be aware of them in case difficulties occur. It is important that you don't assume the worst and that you give your 'awkward customer' the benefit of the doubt. Always seek an explanation for such people's behaviour before you engage in any of the above techniques.

3.5 NERVES

ACTIVITY

What kinds of situations make you nervous? How does your nervousness affect how you speak, stand, come across to others? What effect does it have on your audience?

What have you found in the past to be useful in dealing with nerves? Discuss your own techniques with other presenters. Do they have any other ways of coping with nerves that you would like to try?

When are nerves your friend?

Feeling nervous before your presentation is normal and shows you care about doing a good job. Nerves can have a positive effect by releasing adrenalin into your bloodstream, which will provide you with additional energy and vigour.

Nerves are often born out of a fear of some kind. Listed below are some of the more common types of fears quoted by facilitators:

- Fear of drying up or losing track
- Fear of equipment not working

- Worry that you will not be able to answer any of the audience's questions
- Fear that people will be able to see you are nervous
- Fear that you will have an 'awkward customer'.

Proper preparation beforehand will ensure that most of these will not happen. Even if you do drop your notes, for example, provided you have numbered them you will quickly recover your place. This can also be an ideal opportunity to introduce a long pause and to smile! You can even make a joke at your own expense.

This can win the audience's empathy and relax everyone. After all, you are only human and your audience will not be expecting you to be perfect.

Remember, it is not what goes wrong that matters but how you deal with it.

As for showing your nerves, only a small proportion of the audience will notice and they may well be feeling more anxious than you are. Remember that, for the most part, your audience will look upon you as the expert and won't ever consider that you may be lacking in confidence.

Furthermore, while techniques have been mentioned to help you cope with an 'awkward customer', in reality very few people will set out to ruin your presentation.

Overcoming 'nerves'

You may have your own special rituals or ways of overcoming nerves. If you don't, the following are some techniques that you might find useful to try half-an-hour before your presentation is due to begin:

- *Relaxation techniques* – You may use these in other contexts but if you do not, one of the easiest techniques is to take a number of slow and deep breaths.

Close your eyes so that you can concentrate solely on your breathing and try to shut out everything else. Listen to the sound of your outward breath and, as you do so, feel your shoulders and the rest of your body become more relaxed.

Alternatively, try gradually tensing up all or part of your body. Tense your muscles as hard as you can and then release them on an outward breath. You should feel all your body's tension slip away. Repeat this a few times until you begin to feel completely relaxed.

Most of us are not that in tune with our bodies and are unaware of which parts are feeling particularly tense. As a result, we tend to tense up a specific part of the body more than others. If you're not sure where your tense spots are, try the above exercise with different parts of your body.

When you've located them, you might just want to concentrate on relaxing those areas from then on.

Don't forget your face, especially around the eyes as this can be a particularly tense area. Slowly massaging your temples while your eyes are closed is another very effective way of relaxing. Alternatively, use the exercise above and screw up all your face for a few seconds and then relax.

Listening to relaxation tapes or soft music, or doing yoga or meditation are also very good ways of relaxing before a presentation.

- *Be organised* – go through your checklist and ensure that you have carried out all the necessary preparations. Knowing that you are well-prepared and have everything organised will help you feel more confident and relaxed.

- *Develop a starting ritual* – if you have a specific routine to follow prior to your presentation, this will help concentrate your mind and give you confidence. Include the relaxation exercises that work for you, as well as any useful reminders – such as to smile, establish eye contact, or talk slowly. Talking too quickly at the beginning of a presentation is often a sign that you are nervous.

It sometimes helps if you write out the first couple of minutes of your presentation in full so that you have the chance to settle in a little and gain your confidence.

Many presenters take a few deep breaths before beginning; others use an imagined starting point on the floor and once they reach this, they view themselves as an actor starting their performance.

- *Visualise success* – this is a technique used particularly by sports people and is popular as a method for problem-solving and for achieving the best performances.

For our purposes it involves your mentally walking through your presentation. Visualise yourself being congratulated on your presentation and then go back through your performance and what you did to make it such a success.

Think about your body language, voice, the words that you used, everything in fact that contributed towards your success.

This technique will help you to focus on what you need to do to be successful.

- *Think of the audience or group as just a collection of individuals* – this is, after all, just what they are. Tell yourself that you are in reality only talking to individuals. There may be a large number of them but this is unimportant, they are still only a collection of individuals.

Try to view your audience as caring people who like you and want you to succeed. This will almost always be the case.

- *Rehearse, rehearse and then- rehearse!* – this is the key to a successful performance and for helping you use your nerves positively.

If you have been through your presentation and begin to know it so well that you require only a cursory glance at your notes, you cannot in reality fail.

Ask a trusted colleague or friend to act as a dummy audience and to give positive criticism. You can also try practising in front of a mirror. Always include at least one rehearsal using your visual aids as this will affect your timings and give you confidence that everything fits together smoothly.

Finally, don't let the fact that you are nervous make you any more nervous. Try to let your nerves help you in a positive rather than a negative way.

3.6 CLOSING YOUR PRESENTATION

Your conclusion is as important as your introduction. Your learners' concentration level will again be high and this is a last opportunity for you to reinforce your main teaching points.

The conclusion needs to:

• Review the main learning or key points – this will help consolidate the learning and bring together all the different parts of the presentation

• Revisit your initial aims and check that these have been successfully met

Good timekeeping is critical and you need to set aside about 5-10 minutes. If you over-run, your conclusion will quickly degenerate into a few rushed words while those in your audience pack their bags or fidget impatiently in their seats.

Where you are reviewing objectives, you may wish to involve the group in this review, particularly where you have been using an interactive approach. This should be done at the start of your conclusion, which will enable you to finish with some closing remarks of your own.

3.7 SUMMARY

ACTIVITY

What have been the main learning points for you in this chapter? How will you put these into practice when you make your next presentation?

What preparation and support will you need to do this? How will you go about achieving both?

You are a critical resource to the learning and communication process and as such need to develop your presentational skills as much as possible.

If you have planned your approach carefully this will release you to concentrate on your delivery of the presentation as well as help you deal with any nerves.

Effective presenters will use their voice, body language and eye contact to ensure their audience is fully involved in the learning experience. You need, therefore, to analyse your performance carefully in each of these areas as well as avoid alienating people through the use of:

- Bad language
- Discriminatory remarks
- Inappropriate language or humour
- Irrelevant content
- Inappropriate style or dress
- Feedback that is directive and doesn't concentrate on observable behaviour or agreed performance criteria
- Irritating habits.

Although most group members will desire a successful and positive learning experience, there are a small number who, for whatever reason, may cause you problems. We have therefore looked at a number of techniques that can defuse the situation, and these include:

- Directing a question to them so that they are encouraged to make a contribution
- Discussing their behaviour with them in private
- Making it clear that you would like them to stop chatting, by pausing or asking them a direct question
- Asking them to help others less knowledgeable than themselves
- Letting the rest of the group deal with the problem.

Every presenter at one time or another will feel nervous about a particular event and this should be viewed as positive. As it is important that you are able to cope effectively with your feelings we have looked at a variety of nerve-reducing techniques, including relaxation exercises, visualising success, how to view your audience, and the benefits of having your own personal opening ritual.

The start and close of a presentation are particularly important as these are the times when the audience or learners will be paying particular attention to what you are saying.

Your introduction should:

- Describe your aims and objectives
- Set the scene
- Introduce youself (and the group where appropriate)
- Gain the audience's attention.

Your conclusion should:

- Review the main learning points
- Review your aims and objectives.

CHAPTER 4:
EVALUATION

4.1 INTRODUCTION

Irrespective of whether you are giving a formal presentation or making an after dinner speech you will want to know how successful you have been. You have, after all, spent considerable time planning and preparing your presentation and it would be unusual if you did not want to know the outcome of all that hard work.

Even if your aim is simply to entertain, you will probably undertake some form of assessment to see if this has been achieved. This process is called evaluation.

Where you have specific learning outcomes you will also want to assess whether your group members are achieving the results you want. This will then give you the opportunity to take remedial action if there appear to be problems.

Evaluation needs to be viewed as an integral part of the presentation and, as such, should be carefully considered at the planning stage itself.

The benefits of evaluation

As managers become more time and cost conscious, there is a growing emphasis on the need for a presentation to be able to show its effectiveness in ways that can be clearly demonstrated or quantified.

There are a number of benefits that an evaluation can bring:

- It will help you to develop your skills as a presenter

- It will help you avoid making the same mistake twice

- It will help you develop future presentations

- You will be able to promote the proven benefits to your business and to future audiences

- It will help you make appropriate improvements

- You will be able to assess the quality and impact of the learning experience.

Having established the benefits of monitoring and evaluation, the remainder of this chapter will consider the main methods that can be used for presentation-type events.

4.2 SELECTING YOUR EVALUATION METHODS

There are a number of ways that you can review the effectiveness of a presentation – both in terms of the learning achieved and the approach taken.

You may previously have used a variety of techniques including:

- Informal chats
- End-of-presentation review
- Personal reflection
- Ongoing questioning
- Group quizzes/tests
- End-of-presentation questionnaires.

Informal chats with a few group members over lunch may seem a rather haphazard technique, but a skilled presenter will find this one of the most useful ways of staying in touch – not only with group members' feelings regarding the presentation but also with how much of the learning is actually being assimilated.

The end-of-presentation review, in which you discuss with the group how the event has gone, is the formal equivalent of the above.

Practical considerations, such as the size of your group and the type of presentation you are running, will obviously dictate whether this method is possible or appropriate.

A review of this type needs to be carefully planned and built into the overall presentation content. If it is not, you will find it degenerates into a last minute discussion, with the group members saying whatever they hope you wish to hear in an attempt to draw things to a close quickly. If you explain the benefits of such a review at the beginning of the event, however, and ensure you have sufficient time and well-thought out questions, this can be a highly effective method of review.

ACTIVITY

Write down some questions that you would like to ask at the end of your next presentation.

Here are a few examples:

What parts of the presentation have you found most beneficial? Why?

What aspects of the event were least useful? Why?

What other areas do you feel should have been included/covered?

Which areas, if any, needn't have been included?

What are your suggestions for how subsequent presentations could be improved?

How appropriate were the methods used to cover the content?

What suggestions do you have for covering the material in other ways?

Whatever questions you decide to use, try to keep them as open as possible and be clear in your own mind why you are asking them.

Personal reflection for a few minutes prior to review is a useful way of ensuring those in the group give some thought to their responses. Some presenters ask for group feedback. If you choose this method, allow plenty of time so that the views of all of the group are voiced.

Questioning is an ongoing method of review that can provide you with instantaneous feedback. This method is more appropriate in presentations where you are inviting audience participation and adopting a more learner-centred approach.

Even in more formal presentations you can use questioning at the end of your initial input as part of the overall review or summary.

It is important that you prepare your main questions to ensure they cover all of the key points of your presentation. They should be designed to produce a full response from the group, for example, open rather than closed questions.

Group quizzes or tests can be a fun way of consolidating and reviewing the main points covered, although again these will be more appropriate for less formal presentations where you are taking a more learner-centred approach.

End-of-presentation questionnaires are also known as 'happy sheets', which gives an indication of the problems that can occur with this particular method. Many group members find it difficult to be critical, or give little thought to their responses.

One method for overcoming this is to ensure you have again emphasised the benefits of the questionnaire and have provided sufficient time for its completion. Some presenters prefer to get the group to fill them in later and send them back at an agreed date. This may require a bit of chasing up on your part but should result in the questionnaires being completed properly.

Whatever you decide, it is important that you know what it is that you are seeking from your end-of-presentation questionnaires. It may be that you have a number of reasons for using them. You may, for example, want some feedback on your own presentation skills as well as general feedback on the learning event itself. Or you may also want to know the learners' views on the learning venue itself.

You may also wish to include a section inviting the group members to consider how they can implement the learning points covered.

Finally, you will have your own thoughts on how well the event went, and you should take these into account.

You do need to exercise caution, however, as it can be tempting to repudiate any comments you may not like. You need to be as objective as possible, therefore, and view any criticism as an opportunity to reflect on ways in which you can improve your performance even further.

4.3 SUMMARY
Evaluation should be an integral part of any presentation and needs to be built in to the overall design of the event at the planning stage.

Evaluation will help you to ensure your group is benefiting as much as possible from the learning experience and will give you necessary feedback on how successful it has been in meeting its aims.

There are various methods for evaluating a presentation and these include:

- Informal chats
- End-of-presentation review
- Personal reflection
- Ongoing questioning
- Group quizzes/tests
- End-of-presentation questionnaires.

The techniques chosen will depend on:

- The size of the group
- The type of presentation
- The approach taken.

CONCLUSION

You will have seen that preparing and delivering a presentation requires careful planning and this may initially appear rather daunting and time-consuming.

With experience, however, you will be able to complete most of the initial stages very quickly and they will gradually become second nature.

Effective planning will give you the confidence to run a successful event and will ensure you have a programme that is clearly related to your audience's needs. By adopting a learner-centred approach wherever possible you will also be providing an environment that is stimulating and conducive to improving the effectiveness of your communication.

Once you have gained confidence in your existing skills, you will be able to go on to explore and experiment with those strategies and approaches with which you are less familiar. To help you achieve this you could make your final Activity the completion of a personal development plan that builds on the key learning points from this Handbook.

A development plan for your use is included overleaf. You may, however, prefer to develop one yourself. If you do, don't forget to include at least one measure for each of your objectives.

This will ensure that you will recognise *when* and *how well* you have achieved them. You should also include a timescale for achieving each objective so that you have a date in the future to aim for.

The development plan asks you to consider what support you will need and how you will go about obtaining it. This is because it may be necessary to enlist other people's help to enable you to achieve success.

You will probably find it very helpful to be able to chat about your progress from time to time, so you might find it useful to discuss your development plan with a colleague, manager or trusted friend.

PERSONAL DEVELOPMENT PLAN

NAME: ....

Personal objectives	Measure	Date	Support required
What do I want to achieve?	How will I know when it is achieved?	By when?	What help do I need/ how will I get it?
1.	....	....	....
....	....	....	....
2.	....	....	....
....	....	....	....
3.	....	....	....
....	....	....	....
4.	....	....	....
....	....	....	....
5.	....	....	....
....	....	....	....
6.	....	....	....
....	....	....	....

Signature: ....

Date: ....